Harness Horses, Bucking Broncos & Pit Ponies

A HISTORY OF HORSE BREEDS

WRITTEN AND ILLUSTRATED BY

JEFF CROSBY AND SHELLEY ANN JACKSON

TUNDRA BOOKS

For the girls that we love so dearly: Harper, the horse lover; McKenna, the trick-rider; and Hadley, the horsing-around-ist gal we know. Ride 'em, Cowgirls!

With special thanks to the ladies that we love so dearly: our moms.
—JC & SAJ

A portion of the proceeds from sales of this book will be donated to animal welfare and rescue organizations.

Published in Canada by Tundra Books,
75 Sherbourne Street, Toronto, Ontario M5A 2P9

Published in the United States by Tundra Books of Northern New York,
P.O. Box 1030, Plattsburgh, New York 12901

Library of Congress Control Number: 2011922893

Library and Archives Canada Cataloguing in Publication

Crosby, Jeff
Harness horses, bucking broncos & pit ponies : a history of horse breeds / by Jeff Crosby and Shelley Ann Jackson.

ISBN 978-0-88776-986-3

1. Horse breeds--Juvenile literature. 2. Horses--Juvenile literature.
I. Jackson, Shelley Ann II. Title.

SF291.C76 2011   j636.1   C2011-901228-6

We acknowledge the financial support of the Government of Canada through the Book Publishing Industry Development Program (BPIDP) and that of the Government of Ontario through the Ontario Media Development Corporation's Ontario Book Initiative. We further acknowledge the support of the Canada Council for the Arts and the Ontario Arts Council for our publishing program.

ONTARIO ARTS COUNCIL
CONSEIL DES ARTS DE L'ONTARIO

Printed and bound in China

1 2 3 4 5 6   16 15 14 13 12 11

Contents

Introduction

No animal has had a greater impact on human civilization than the horse. How did the relationship between humans and horses begin? As far back as 10,000 BC, during the ice age, people hunted horses for food. Their hides were used to make clothing and build shelter, and their bones were made into tools and weapons. Approximately six thousand years later, people living on the steppes of central Asia and eastern Europe began building fences in which to pen horses, to avoid the challenges of following herds to hunt. By penning the herds near their settlements, humans were able to use the horses when they needed them. This was likely the first step toward domestication.

As people kept horse herds, they began to rely more heavily on the animals for their way of life. They used horse dung to insulate the roofs of their homes and to fuel their fires. Horses became part of religious rituals and were sometimes sacrificed. And, as the horses became familiar with their keepers, humans were better able to control them. People discovered that milking the horses could provide their populations with nourishment. Most importantly, people started to select which horses should mate. They probably made this selection based on which animals were least afraid of them. After a few generations, this would have created horses whose temperaments made them easier to handle. This also would have resulted in a variety of coat colors and markings, because gentleness and appearance are genetically linked. (When an animal becomes tame, its hormone levels change. Over generations, the different hormones affect the animals' appearances. Rather than the homogeneity of the wild herd, the domesticated animals may develop a variety of coat colors, features, and markings.)

An animal is considered *domestic* when its offspring naturally look and behave differently than the young of its wild ancestors. Like other animals that have been successfully domesticated, horses are social animals. They live in family groups and follow a social *hierarchy*, meaning that younger or submissive horses will follow older or more dominant horses and that there is only one herd leader. In the wild, these behaviors help them to stay safe from predators, such as wolves and mountain lions. But in domestic environments, it means that horses are trainable because they will follow the commands of a human leader.

Not long after domestication, humans probably began riding horses. It might have been necessary to jump onto the back of a lead horse, controlling it with a rope around the jaw, in order to direct the herd. Early domestic horses were also harnessed to pull carts and chariots. For the first time, humans had a reliable, speedy form of transportation. Knowledge, culture, and religion spread as horse people expanded and explored. Raiding neighboring villages was a simpler task on horseback, and societies with horses had an advantage over those without. The outcome of wars became dependant on horses and the skill of an army's mounted warriors. With a horse, work of all types could be done more quickly and with less difficulty. And to fill their free moments, people developed *equine* (horse-related) sports.

By *natural selection*, horses that were better adapted to a particular environment survived to pass their traits on to their offspring. But with *artificial selection*, humans chose which horses reproduced, thereby bringing out certain features to suit their needs. A group of horses that is bred over time to have a select set of characteristics is called a *breed*. People have created horse breeds to be different than their ancestors. Some are smaller and gentler, swifter and nimbler, or more massive and strong – some even have a particular coat color or texture.

Today, there are over two hundred recognized breeds of horses. Because there are so many, they are not all described in this book. Often horses are divided into categories by size. *Heavy horses* are big and muscular, used for agriculture and *draft* work (pulling loads). *Light horses* are lean and narrow and are put to work with carriages or under saddle. *Ponies* are stocky horses under fifteen hands high, often made small by the poor conditions in which they live. But because the focus of this book is the history of horse breeds, the forty-three breeds you will read about here are organized by original purpose, beginning with the horse's oldest job and progressing to the most modern. You will see how each breed's history has influenced the way it looks and behaves today.

THOROUGHBRED

KNABSTRUPPER

FALABELLA

NORWEGIAN FJORD

NORTH AMERICAN
CURLY HORSE

SHIRE

—20 HH
—19 HH
—18 HH
—17 HH
—16 HH
—15 HH
—14 HH
—13 HH
—12 HH
—11 HH
—10 HH
—9 HH
—8 HH
—7 HH
—6 HH
—5 HH
—4 HH
—3 HH
—2 HH
—1 HH
—0 HH

SHETLAND

9

Rapid Transit

After the horse was domesticated, the first job it was trained to do was provide transportation. The horse was chosen over other domestic animals because of its speed. Wild horses need to be fast to outrun predators. They also don't have to rest while digesting food, like cows and camels do, and they eat a diet of only grass. So horses can travel continuously and can go virtually anywhere. In addition, horses have tremendous strength and *stamina*, which means they can work all day without resting. With horses, it was less effort for people to follow their prey, search for food and water, and carry their belongings. For four thousand years, the horse was the most rapid, dependable form of transportation.

THE ARABIAN, ONE OF THE EARLIEST BREEDS.

Early domestic horses transported people by pulling a wheeled vehicle, such as a cart or chariot, or by horseback, depending on the terrain. In the desert, it was necessary to ride horses because wheels would get stuck in sand or gravel. But a swift horse could travel through this uneven landscape more quickly and manageably. Desert breeds developed features to help them cope in this harsh climate, such as fine, well-veined skin for rapid heat loss, an attribute known as *dry skin*.

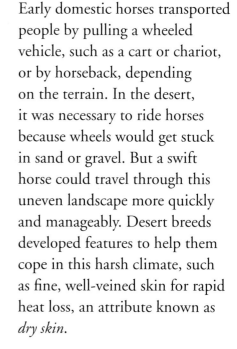

THE BARB, A DESERT HORSE.

Riding horses was also crucial in mountain areas, where paths were too steep, narrow, and rocky for vehicles. Sure-footed horses became an essential part of life in these areas. Horses bred for mountain use have special physical adaptations too, such as ample hearts and lungs, hard hooves, and sickle-shaped legs, which help with balance.

A *gait* is one of the ways that a horse moves. Walk, trot, canter, and gallop are gaits that all horses perform naturally. Some horses also have an *ambling gait*, a special movement that smoothes out the ride over rough terrain. These breeds are called *gaited*. Gaited breeds inherit their ambling gaits naturally or are able to learn them with minimal training. Riders prefer gaited horses on long or rocky trails.

THE KABARDIN, A MOUNTAIN BREED.

THE MISSOURI FOX TROTTER, A GAITED BREED.

THE KLADRUBY, A CARRIAGE HORSE.

The first domesticated horses were somewhat small and difficult to ride. But if two or more were harnessed to a wheeled vehicle, their combined strengths could pull riders and their supplies. In areas where the terrain would allow it, this was the favored way to utilize the horse's power. Over time, carriage horses were bred to be bigger and stronger so that they could pull heavier vehicles and loads. Before they were replaced by railroads during the Industrial Revolution, horse-drawn coaches were the main source of transportation for peoples living in Europe and the Americas.

Arabian

The Arabian Horse originated on the Arabian Peninsula around 2500 BC. There, the nomadic bedu tribes bred Arabian Horses for riding in the desert. Arabians carried the bedouins vast distances in search of food and water, so they evolved into horses of incredible stamina. To cope with desert life, Arabians have "dry skin" and a *jibbah*, extra sinus space that cools hot desert air and causes a slight bulge on the forehead. The Arabian is different from most horses in that it has one less lumbar vertebra, one less pair of ribs, and two less tailbones. This is why the Arabian carries its tail high and looks as if it is floating when it moves. It also has a short head, small muzzle, and concave face. When bedouins raided their neighbors, they preferred to ride *mares* (adult female horses) over *stallions* (adult male horses) because mares didn't nicker and alert the enemy while approaching. For long treks, the bedouins still utilized the camel for transportation. In the sixth century, the Prophet Muhammad, founder of the Islamic religion, led his armies on religious conquests. It was then that the emphasis moved to the horse, a faster, more reliable animal. During his conquests, Muhammad introduced the breed to north Africa and the Middle East. The influential Arabian Horse is the founder of more breeds than any other horse.

Fast as the wind. Bedouin legend says that God created the Arabian from a handful of south wind, and gave to it flight without wings. Arabs consider the horse to be the lord of all animals, and the Arabian to be the most revered breed.

EUROPE

AFRICA Arabian Peninsula

Indian Ocean

13

Barb

The Barb comes from the Barbary Coast of Africa. It is an ancient breed of horse raised by the nomadic Berber tribes. Like the Arabian, the Barb is a desert horse and shares some of the same features. It is very hardy and has excellent resistance to heat and drought. It also has the lean, tough build of a desert horse and "dry skin" for quick cooling. Despite these similarities, the Barb does not resemble the Arab in appearance. Its head is long and its profile is straight or convex, known as a *ram's head*. The Barb has sloping quarters and its tail carries low. During the seventh and eighth centuries, Muslim armies conquered north Africa on their Arabian Horses. There was some crossing of the two breeds at that time, but the Barb's features are more *dominant*, or stronger, so the Barb's look did not change. After the Berber people converted to Islam, they joined the conquests and invaded Spain. For the Muslim warriors, the Arabian was a treasured horse, while the Barb was a valuable fighting horse. When the Barb traveled to Spain in the early eighth century, it became a foundation for many Spanish and European breeds.

Within arm's reach. Barb Horses were experts at the *jineta* style of riding, in which the horse anticipated the mounted warrior's needs and put him in position to use his weapons effectively. Fighting was done in close combat during these times, with the rider relying on both the Barb's agility to quickly maneuver and on its courage to remain in the action.

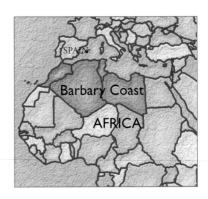

Icelandic Horse

When the Norse settlers, or Vikings, first arrived in Iceland over a thousand years ago, they brought along their small, sturdy horses. There were no native peoples to conquer, just inhospitable land. The Vikings relied on their horses to transport belongings and supplies, and to do the heavy work required to build their settlements. They rode the horses vast distances over the cold, rugged island. Since cattle couldn't survive in the freezing climate, these horses also became a source of food. Natural selection played a big role in the development of the Icelandic Horse. It became an extremely hardy breed, because only the toughest horses could survive the long arctic winters while grazing just on sparse grasses. It also developed a double coat to protect it from the cold. There are no predators of horses in Iceland, so Icelandic Horses are known for being less spooky than other breeds. The Icelandic Horse is a rare five-gaited horse. This means that it is able to master five different gaits: walk, trot, canter, pace, and the unique *tölt* (a very fluid gait). This ability makes the breed very versatile and allows these horses to move comfortably over different terrains at varying speeds.

Fight club! To determine breeding to fight each other. This fighting became a form of entertainment for the settlers as well as a popular social event where disagreements were settled, political alliances were formed, and young men and women courted.

Kabardin

The Kabardin (pronounced KAH-ber-deen) developed in the northern Caucasus Mountains of central Asia in the sixteenth century. The area's nomadic mountain tribesmen used it as a saddle horse and packhorse. They also rode the Kabardin when tending their herds of sheep and goats. The tribesmen selectively bred the Kabardin for one main feature: the ability to survive in extreme mountain conditions. The Kabardin accumulates fat quickly, which insulates it against the cold, and its blood processes oxygen more efficiently than other horses, improving its capacity for working at high altitudes. The Kabardin has sickle-shaped back legs for balance. The movement of its legs is high and energetic for traversing through rocky terrain. Its extremely hard hooves are rarely *shod*, or fit with horseshoes. The Kabardin's thick, powerful build allows it to carry a rider over great distances through rugged mountains in deep snow. Because it is sure-footed and calm-tempered, it can safely canter or trot downhill and does not panic when stones roll underfoot. Snow, rain, hail, and torrential streams don't bother this breed, and it can find its way through mist and darkness, conditions that might otherwise disorient a rider.

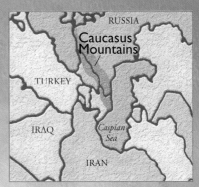

King of the mountain. Many of the features that make the Kabardin a supreme mountain horse would be considered defects in another breed. The Kabardin will not win any races — except, perhaps, a race to the top of the mountain.

Peruvian Paso

When Francisco Pizarro and the Spanish conquistadores arrived in Peru in the early sixteenth century, they brought with them Spanish horses. In their new home, these horses were selectively bred to become superb mountain riding horses. *Paso* (pronounced PAH-so) means "step" and refers to the breed's unique ambling gait, during which the hooves on one side of the body hit the ground at the same time, then the hooves on the other side. This ambling gait has an uncommon feature called *termino*, in which the feet swing outward with each step, keeping the rider steady no matter how rocky the terrain. Every purebred Peruvian Paso foal inherits this gait and no training is necessary. The Paso has a long stride, which is essential for traveling great distances through the Andes mountains. Another feature that makes the Peruvian Paso an excellent mountain horse is its extra-large heart and strong lungs, an adaptation for working in the thin mountain air. The Paso is good at climbing, thanks to its hard hooves and bones. The Peruvian Paso also has *mountain sense*, which means it stays calm and smart even when journeying through narrow, rocky mountain paths. Today, this national horse of Peru is not only popular in its native country, but also in the United States and Columbia.

Champagne ride. A ride on the back of a Peruvian Paso is so smooth it is known as the "champagne ride." A rider can literally carry a flute filled with champagne without even spilling one drop!

Appaloosa

The Appaloosa is named after the Palouse River in the American Northwest, the valleys of which provided year-round protection and food for this breed. The Nez Percé tribe developed the Appaloosa breed in the mid-1700s from descendents of horses introduced to the Americas by Spanish conquistadores. Horses changed the Nez Percé culture forever, giving them not only mobility, but also power. From sedentary fishermen, the Nez Percé became nomadic buffalo hunters, trading buffalo hides for goods and living in transportable tepees. They were the only Native Americans to practice strict selective breeding with their horses. Though Appaloosas also exist with solid-colored coats, the Nez Percé prized Appaloosas with spotted coats because these provided both decoration and camouflage.

A horse of many colors. Appaloosas are known for their unique coat patterns: leopard (white with dark spots), snowflake (dark with white spots), blanket (dark with a white rectangle covering the hips, with or without spots), marbleized (a mixture of colors), and frost (dark with white spots on hips).

CANADA

UNITED STATES OF AMERICA

Washington

Palouse River

Oregon

The whites of an Appaloosa's eyes are more prominent than in other breeds, and its hooves have vertical stripes. The breed was almost destroyed in 1877 when the United States Army forcibly removed the Nez Percé from their land. The tribe fought back but eventually surrendered, at which time the army slaughtered most of their horses, to keep the Nez Percé from fighting again. The Appaloosa Horse Club revived the breed in 1938. Today, the Appaloosa is one of the most popular breeds in the United States, with over sixty-five thousand registered horses.

Missouri Fox Trotter

In the 1820s, American pioneers moved west from their homes on the hills and plantations of Kentucky, Tennessee, and Virginia to settle the Ozark Mountains of Missouri and Arkansas, bringing their saddle horses with them. In the Ozarks, they bred these horses to carry them through the rocky, forest-covered hills. They soon found that the best horses for this type of riding moved with a *fox trot* and they began selectively breeding them for this gait. In a fox trot, the horse appears to walk with its front feet and trot with its back feet. The back feet stay low to the ground and almost slide forward, so the ride is very smooth and comfortable for the rider. The Missouri Fox Trotter, as it became known, can travel great distances while trotting at a speed of five to eight miles (8 to 13 km) per hour. Even today it is a popular mount for long-distance trail rides. It's easy to recognize this sure-footed horse as it trots: head to tail, its whole body moves rhythmically and smoothly.

So fast it's a sin! Though some of the breeds that combined to create the Missouri Fox Trotter were speedy racehorses, such as the Thoroughbred and Standard-bred, Puritan religious beliefs considered racing to be frivolous and — therefore — a sin. The settlers instead bred their Fox Trotters to be calm, gentle riding horses.

Three-horse sleigh. Orlov Trotters are famous for pulling Russian *troikas*. A troika is a traditional Russian sled led by three horses harnessed side by side. The center horse trots while the two outside horses, which are harnessed at an angle, must canter or gallop to keep up.

RUSSIA

• Khrenovsky Stud

Orlov Trotter

Catherine the Great of Russia gave an expansive piece of land to Count Alexei Orlov to thank him for taking part in the assassination of Paul III, which brought her to the throne. It was on this land that the count built the Khrenovsky *stud* (a stable or farm where stallions are kept for breeding). In 1778, the count set out to create a light harness horse of exceptional speed, stamina, and beauty. Because of his considerable wealth, the count was able to keep as many as three thousand horses at once, importing fine specimens from all over Europe and Asia. He experimented with different combinations of these horses until he developed the ideal Russian trotting horse. Servants cared for the horses and kept meticulous breeding and performance records. Only the most beautiful horses with the fastest trots were selected to breed. The Russian climate is quite severe, so mares and their foals were kept outside to ensure their hardiness. By the early nineteenth century, Orlov Trotters were well-known competitors in Moscow trotting races, which were usually held in winter with the horses pulling sleighs. This breed was also used on farms and for drawing carriages and Russian *troikas*. The Orlov Trotter is a tall but light horse with a long neck and back.

Kladruby

In 1562, the Holy Roman Emperor Maximilian II created a horse stud at Kladruby nad Labem (now part of the Czech Republic). Seventeen years later, his successor King Rudolf II elevated the stud's status to Imperial Court Stud Farm to develop a breed of horses to pull the splendid ceremonial carriages of the Austrian Court. The state breeders used Spanish and Italian horses to create the Kladruby breed. The Kladruby is a heavy carriage horse with a broad, muscular build. It has a ram's-head profile, small ears, and a swan-like neck. The carriages that these horses pulled are known as *four-* or *six-in-hand* carriages. This means that, with special rigging, one person drove a carriage pulled by four or six horses. Originally, Kladrubers came in all colors, but the imperial court in Vienna required that eighteen black and eighteen white stallions were kept on hand at all times. Black horses were used for religious ceremonies and white horses were used for all other events. As a result of this color preference, only white and black Kladrubers are bred today. Though the breed is over four hundred years old, it is one of the rarest. Due to war, political upheaval in the country, and lack of interest in the breed, there are only about seven hundred black and white Kladrubers in the Czech Republic today. They are mainly used for sport driving.

Gypsy Vanner

The Romani people, often called Gypsies, are nomads who originated in India and traveled about Europe in their colorful covered wagons, known as *caravans*. For centuries, Gypsies of eastern Europe bred horses to pull these caravans. But these horses were not considered a distinct breed until 1996, when the Gypsy Vanner breed registry was created. Though Gypsies don't travel in caravans anymore, the Gypsy Vanner is still bred with the same goal in mind: to create the perfect caravan horse. The standards for such a horse were set in the Gypsy community's oral traditions rather than passed down through written documentation. Originally created from a variety of draft horses, Gypsy Vanners have stocky, powerful builds with short necks and backs, features that enable them to pull the heavy wagons. Because they have abundant stamina and calm personalities, they are easy to maintain and travel with. The horses, bred to be as colorful as the caravans themselves, come mostly in *piebald* (black and white) or *skewbald* (brown and white). Their manes and tails are long and flowing. When running, the heavy feathering on their feet gives Gypsy Vanners the appearance of flying.

Drum horse. The Queen of England's procession uses horses that carry heavy silver kettle drums and that are steered by reigns attached to the feet of the drummers, who are riding the horses. Horses of any breed can become drum horses if they are strong enough to carry rider and drums, if they are attractive, and if they are sufficiently calm to walk through parade crowds with beating drums on their backs. In 2006, the American Drum Horse Association began registering Drum Horses. Like the Gypsy Vanner, a new breed was created based on the qualities required of a horse for this longstanding job.

Military Advantage

Not long after they began riding horses, horse cultures saw the military advantage they had over non-horse cultures. Though early horses were small, their strength and speed made them invaluable. Many ancient cultures used teams of two to four horses to pull two-wheeled chariots, each ridden by a driver and one or more soldiers, who loosed arrows or spears on the enemy as the chariot sped by.

THE CASPIAN, A CHARIOT HORSE.

THE MONGOLIAN, A LIGHT CAVALRY HORSE.

In most ancient cultures, *cavalry*, or mounted soldiers, scouted, harassed the enemy with quick attacks, and chased retreating enemies, while foot soldiers did the majority of fighting. Some armies, though, were composed entirely of cavalry. They could move their whole force rapidly, surprising and outmaneuvering the enemy. These cavalry horses were light and built for speed and endurance.

24

The strategy of using heavily armored knights to fight on horseback began in medieval Europe. This type of cavalry charged in tight formations, crashing straight into the enemy, lances first. This tactic required large, strong horses that could carry fully armored knights and their gear, and that were also courageous and willing to charge head-on into danger. The widespread use of firearms and artillery in the sixteenth century brought about the end of the age of the mounted knight.

THE SHIRE, A HEAVY CAVALRY HORSE.

THE FRIESIAN, A BREED THAT PULLED ARTILLERY IN WORLD WAR II.

Horses had long been used in military baggage trains to pull wagons of food, gear, and ammunition to the front lines. They also hauled heavy artillery into battle and carted the wounded out. With their strength and calm demeanors, heavy draft horses were the ultimate horses for this role.

Caspian

The Caspian is the oldest domestic breed of horse, depicted in ancient Persian art as far back as 3000 BC. It lived in Persia, now Iran, south of the Caspian Sea. The Caspian was too small for comfortable riding, but teams of two or four were used to pull chariots for hunting, racing, and war. In warfare, soldiers protected themselves with shields while throwing spears or shooting arrows from the chariot. Often the chariot was *scythed*, having blades that jut out from the sides. The Caspian was thought to have died out in the seventh century. But in 1965, it was rediscovered in mountainous northwest Iran, where locals were using the animal to pull carts. This miniature horse, standing ten to thirteen hands high, links primitive horses to desert breeds such as the Arabian. Its skeletal structure is primitive, with a jibbah, an extra pair of molars in the upper jaw, oval-shaped hooves, and broad *scapulas* (shoulder blades). Yet its other features are remarkably similar to the Arabian (which also has a jibbah): wide nostrils, a small muzzle, "dry skin," and a long, flowing mane and tail. Today's Caspian performs well in harness and driving competitions, perhaps due to its chariot-pulling ancestors.

End of an era. At the Battle of Gaugamela (in present day Iraq) in 331 BC, Alexander the Great tried a new tactic against the armies of Darius III. Rather than fighting the two hundred Persian scythed chariots head on, the Macedonian army's front lines stepped aside, letting them pass. The Macedonians then attacked the chariots from behind and defeated them. This marked the end of Persian chariot warfare.

IRAQ

IRAN

Caspian Sea

Mongolian

The Mongolian Horse is an ancient breed that made its mark in the twelfth century as the steed of Genghis Khan's nomadic warrior tribes. These Mongolian warriors conquered nations across Asia and eastern Europe for over a hundred years, creating the largest contiguous empire in the history of the world. They achieved all of this on the backs of their small but quick and tough horses. A Mongolian warrior practically lived in the saddle. He controlled his horse with his legs and by shifting his body weight. While riding, he could shoot arrows in all directions, including backward. Mongolian warriors scouted the enemy's position and numbers on horseback beforehand, so they knew exactly how and where to attack. They outmaneuvered and defeated their opponents by using complex flag signals on horseback. If they desperately needed nourishment, they pricked the necks of their horses and drank the blood without seriously damaging the animals. The Mongolian Horse is very hardy, surviving on minimal food and water. It lives without shelter in harsh climates, such as the Gobi desert, where its dense fur is its only protection. The Mongolian Horse is compact, with a short, strong neck, a heavy head, and sturdy legs.

Horse country. In Mongolia today, there are over three million Mongolian Horses. That's more horses living in the country than people! Many of the country's citizens are still nomads, relying on their horses for transportation, yak herding, meat, and milk. Some also enjoy using their horses for races and games of polo.

Norwegian Fjord

The Norwegian Fjord Horse and its ancestors have lived in Norway for four thousand years. For the last two thousand of those, they were selectively bred, as shown by carved images found at Viking burial sites. The Vikings rode the Fjord into battle, and when they began raiding Scotland's Western Isles in 1150, the horses traveled with them in their open longboats. The animals were also used in the bloody sport of horse fighting for the entertainment of the Vikings. The Fjord is one of the few breeds of horse that very closely resemble primitive horses. It is thick and muscular but also small and agile. Fjords are always dun colored with a black "eel" stripe running down the spine from forelock to tail. *Zebra bars*, or zebra-like stripes, are often present on the legs. The mane, which has silver outer hairs and black center hairs, is coarse and stands erect. The Fjord is sure-footed, brave, and hardy enough to endure the cold, wet weather of its northern home. Today, the Fjord still works in Norway, plowing fields and pulling loads on the hilly farms.

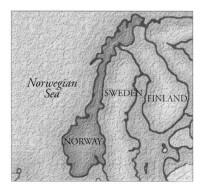

Ancient hairstyle? If left alone, the Norwegian Fjord's mane would grow as long as any other horse's. But it is an ancient tradition to clip it short, as seen in carvings on Viking *rune-stones*, or commemorative stones decorated with inscriptions. The black hairs are cut to stand above the silver ones, exaggerating the curve of the horse's neck.

29

Andalusian

The word *Andalusian* refers to an area of southern Spain. In its homeland, the Andalusian Horse is known as the *Pura Raza Española*, or "Pure Spanish Race." Horses have lived on the Iberian Peninsula since at least 25,000 BC. The Andalusian is a descendent of these Iberian horses. As far back as 2000 BC, when the Phoenicians arrived in Iberia, the Iberian army was already known for its powerful cavalry. The many invading armies that passed through Iberia praised the horse as a warhorse without equal. In medieval times, knights wore heavy armor, which created the need for a larger, stronger horse, and the Andalusian's popularity decreased. But once firearms were invented and the armored knight was outmoded, the Andalusian again gained favor. It was the warhorse of choice from the fifteenth to the eighteenth century. The conquistadores rode this breed in their invasions of the Americas. Although it is not the fastest of horses, the Andalusian is a very strong, agile animal, allowing it to perform maneuvers on the battlefield that are needed by a mounted soldier. It is a proud, brave horse, yet it is also gentle and affectionate toward people. The Andalusian is typically bay or gray, and its ram's head – long, with a straight or convex profile – is shaped similar to the Barb. It has a very long, thick, often wavy mane and tail.

The lord's horse. The Spanish hero El Cid, meaning "The Lord," battled atop his famous Andalusian, named Babieca, for thirty years. El Cid died while fighting at Valencia in 1099. By El Cid's last order, his dead body was fastened into Babieca's saddle and the horse led the troops into battle, thus ending the Moors' seven-hundred-year occupation of Spain.

Atlantic Ocean

FRANCE

SPAIN

Iberian Peninsula

Mediterranean Sea

AFRICA

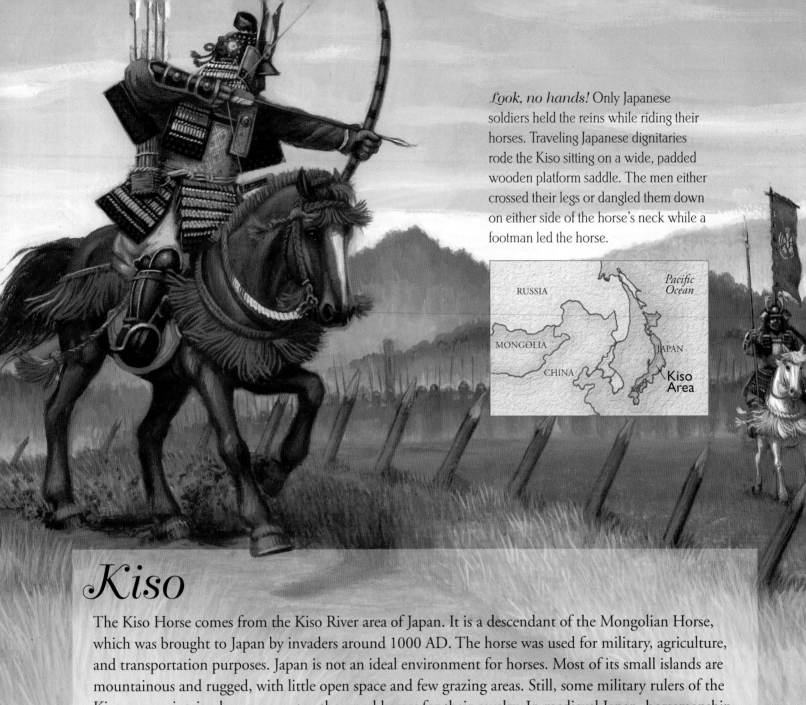

Look, no hands! Only Japanese soldiers held the reins while riding their horses. Traveling Japanese dignitaries rode the Kiso sitting on a wide, padded wooden platform saddle. The men either crossed their legs or dangled them down on either side of the horse's neck while a footman led the horse.

RUSSIA

Pacific Ocean

MONGOLIA

CHINA

JAPAN

Kiso Area

Kiso

The Kiso Horse comes from the Kiso River area of Japan. It is a descendant of the Mongolian Horse, which was brought to Japan by invaders around 1000 AD. The horse was used for military, agriculture, and transportation purposes. Japan is not an ideal environment for horses. Most of its small islands are mountainous and rugged, with little open space and few grazing areas. Still, some military rulers of the Kiso area maintained as many as ten thousand horses for their cavalry. In medieval Japan, horsemanship was a key part of a warrior's training to become a samurai knight. A samurai had to be able to shoot a bow and arrow while riding a horse into battle. From this skill, a sport called *yabusame* developed, in which riders shoot arrows at a target from the back of a galloping horse. In the nineteenth century, the Japanese fought against several Western countries and admired their opponents' larger, stronger horses. The military began crossing the Kiso with outside breeds to improve their fighting capabilities. This, combined with the replacement of horses by machines on farms and roads, nearly wiped out the purebred Kiso. There are less than a hundred of these horses living today, registered and preserved in Japan.

Basotho

In 1652, the Dutch East India Company started settlements in South Africa near the Cape of Good Hope. These settlers imported horses, animals never seen before by the native people of the Cape. These horses developed into a breed called the Cape Horse. In 1822, the Zulu tribe began raiding the farms of the *Boers*, or Dutch farmers, and stealing their Cape Horses. This marks the first time that South African tribesmen owned horses. A period of invasions and wars between South African tribes followed, and, in 1829, the Basotho tribe, living in what is now known as Lesotho, gained their first horse. They, in turn, began raiding their neighbors, taking horses for their own, until the whole tribe was mounted. The Basotho nation then had a huge military advantage over their horseless neighbors. The tribesmen rode their sure-footed steeds fast and fearlessly down the steep mountain slopes. Through natural selection, the Basotho breed became very hardy. They lived without shelter and grazed for all of their food. To adapt to the high altitude, they developed strong hearts and lungs; and for crossing the steep, rocky terrain, they developed sturdy legs with hard hooves.

Bought out? The Basotho was such a hardy breed that the British military bought thirty thousand of them as warhorses for the Anglo-Boer War in the late nineteenth century. Unfortunately, they took the best of the breed and left only the most inferior animals with the Basotho nation. Efforts have been made in modern times to restore the Basotho to its best form in South Africa.

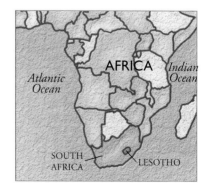

Marwari

Throughout much of India's early history, its many principalities warred with each other. In the thirteenth century, the Rathores, the traditional rulers of Kanauj, were forced from their kingdom and lost their land. They fled to the deserts of northwest India with their horses, to a region called Marwar, which translates into "land of death." There, they bred the Marwari Horse. The Rathores selected their horses for the ability to exist in this harsh land, with its shifting sand dunes, scorching heat, and limited food and water. The horses were vital to the Rathores survival: they had to travel long distances quickly between settlements, and they were ridden as battle horses for the Rathore cavalry. Famous for their loyalty, they were known to carry their wounded masters home from the battlefield. The Marwari is a strong, wiry horse. The unique slant of its shoulder bones enables it to move easily through deep sand. Its hooves are so hard they are rarely shod. The Marwari's most distinctive feature is its very mobile ears, which curve toward each other, the tips often touching. It is said to have superb hearing, giving horse and rider early warning of danger.

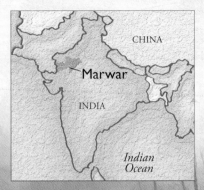

Chetak attack. A famous legend tells of Maharana Pratap and his Marwari, Chetak. While attacking an enemy commander who rode an elephant, Chetak jumped so high that Pratap was able to strike the commander with his lance. Though Chetak was wounded, he leaped over a gorge to escape, then died in his master's arms.

Shire

Pulling it's own weight – and more! The massive Shire weighs more than a ton. It is muscular and broad, with wide hooves that provide greater traction for pulling. In 1954, using their incredible strength, a pair of Shires pulled a weight of forty-five tons (40.8 metric tons) in a competition. That is equal to the weight of about eighteen cars!

The Shire is a descendant of the heavy medieval warhorse known as the English Great Horse. Great Horses bravely charged into battle carrying fully armored knights. To carry a knight, his armor, and his weapons, these horses had to be massive and strong, yet they were not the giants that Shires are today. When the times of tournaments and armored knights passed (by the seventeenth century), the English used Great Horses to pull plows on farms and haul heavy wagons over the rough roads. Through the years, other heavy horses were imported to England for work and were bred with the Great Horse. In the nineteenth century, in several *shires*, or counties, of England, these horses lugged burdensome loads through marshland and clay soils. This was tiring work, so breeders began selectively breeding for even larger and more powerful horses – the final step in creating the modern Shire: the world's strongest, heaviest, and tallest horse. After World War II, with the increased use of machines, the breed severely declined, as did most draft horse breeds. Today, Shires have regained popularity, and the Shire can be found mainly in the United Kingdom, the United States, and Canada, pulling brewery wagons and plows, clearing trees in the forestry industry, and competing in weight-pulling contests.

Friesian

Seamen, farmers, and horse breeders settled Friesland of the northern Netherlands in 500 BC. They raised the ancestors of the Friesian (pronounced FREE-zhen), which came to be recognized as a respected warhorse. The Frieslanders rode their Friesian Horses into war with the Roman legions when they invaded Britain. In the sixteenth century, during the Crusades of the Middle Ages, German and Friesian knights chose this strong, compact horse in war against the Muslims in the Middle East. It was able to carry an incredible amount of weight but still maneuver quickly. It was also a practical and docile horse, easy to maintain and handle. The elegant Friesian is known for its high stepping trot, sometimes brushing its own elbows with its front heels. When the Spanish occupied the Netherlands during the Eighty Years' War, some Andalusian traits were introduced into the Friesian. This is why its long black mane and tail have a distinctive waviness. The Friesian is a good trotter, which almost led to its demise. In the early twentieth century, trotting races became popular, and the Friesian was mixed with other breeds to produce a lighter, faster horse. Only a handful of pure Friesians remained. But during World War II, because of limited fuel and machinery, there was a return to horsepower and the traditional Friesian was revived.

Hearse horse. With its solid black coat, proud bearing, and stylish trot, the Friesian is the favored breed for pulling hearses in traditional funerals in England.

Trakehner

In the thirteenth century, to convert locals to Christianity, the Order of the Teutonic Knights colonized East Prussia, which is now part of Poland. They began a horse-breeding program to produce strong, hardy military horses, using native (now extinct) Schweiken ponies as a base. Five hundred years later, in 1732, King Friedrich Wilhelm I of Prussia founded a stud farm to shape these horses to the needs of the Prussian cavalry. The breed is called Trakehners (pronounced tra-KAY-ners) after the Trakehnen stud, which was established on drained marshland. This proved to be some of the best country for breeding horses. It had lush pastures, wide open space, and a good climate. The Royal Trakehnen Stud Administration focused on refining the line with very selective breeding and testing. It produced cavalry mounts for the Prussian army, as well as fast and elegant carriage horses for nobility. During World War I, the Trakehner was the warhorse of choice; its large size, strength, and agility, plus its calm, courageous behavior, made it invaluable in battle. These same qualities make it an excellent competition horse today. The Trakehner dominated the 1936 Berlin Olympic Games, winning almost every medal in the *equestrian*, or horseback-riding, events.

Terrible trek. In 1944, near the end of World War II, the Russian army advanced on Poland. After evacuating Trakehnen Stud, the Poles hitched their horses to wagons filled with their belongings. Most horses were captured. The eight hundred that escaped had to walk six hundred miles (966 km) through the bitter winter cold to western Germany. Less than a hundred Trakehners survived the trek.

North Sea

Baltic Sea

Trakehnen Stud

GERMANY

POLAND

EUROPE

Horsepower

Before the invention of the automobile, the easiest way to move a heavy load was to use a draft animal, often a horse. No matter their size, these horses had to have extreme strength and endurance to move their cargo, which they either carried on their backs or pulled in carts, wagons, or other vehicles.

THE CLYDESDALE, A DRAFT BREED.

THE CONNEMARA, A FARM HORSE.

On farms, draft animals hauled plows and carted crops. In the eleventh century, as large European warhorses became obsolete on the battlefield, these too were put to work in the fields (although oxen were still the preferred farm draft animal until the 1700s, when innovations in farm machinery required the faster, even pace of the horse). Farm horses needed to be big, strong, docile, and willing to work all day.

When colonists settled new areas around the world, they usually brought horses with them. It was necessary that the animals survive not only the long journey, often over rough seas, but also the climate and conditions of the new land. These hardy horses were all-purpose and used for a variety of jobs, such as clearing land, working farms, drawing carriages, and lugging goods.

THE CANADIAN HORSE, A VERSATILE COLONIST BREED.

THE CAMARGUE, A HERDING BREED.

Horses are also useful for herding. Atop a horse, a herdsman or cowboy has a higher vantage point for observing stock. A rider can use the mass of the horse to block animals from straying and the speed of the horse to outrun them. Skilled horses are said to have *cow sense*, or the ability to read a cow's behavior and predict its movements.

Shetland

The Shetland Pony comes from the Shetland Islands off of the north coast of Scotland. It has existed there for thousands of years, probably crossing over from mainland Europe before mainland Europe was separated from the British Isles by water. Harsh weather, a lack of natural shelter, and just tough grasses and seaweed for food make the Shetland Islands a hard place for horses to live. This is the reason the Shetland, smallest of the pony breeds, is so diminutive. Despite their size, the ponies are unusually strong. Shetland farmers used them from ancient times until modern times as packhorses, to carry heavy loads of peat from the hills to be used as fuel for kitchen fires, and to cart seaweed inland from the coast for fertilizer. The ponies could also carry grown men for long distances. Known as "Scotland's Little Giant," the five- to six-hundred-pound (227- to 272-kg) Shetland can carry up to half its weight. The Shetland has a thick tail and mane, along with a dense, shaggy coat to protect it from the cold, wet weather of its home. These ponies are popular as pets and children's mounts because of their small size and cute appearance.

Pit ponies. The Industrial Revolution brought about a massive demand for coal. When an 1847 law forbade women and children from working in the filthy, dangerous coal mines, Shetland Ponies took their place. These pit ponies were small enough to fit down the low, narrow shafts, yet strong enough to pull out bulky carts of coal.

American Miniature

Miniature horses differ from ponies in their proportions. Ponies have short legs, a boxy head, and heavy muscling, but miniature horses look like scaled-down versions of regular-sized horses. Miniature horses have existed for centuries. Some were pampered in the royal courts of Europe as pets and curiosities. But others did not live such luxurious lives, working tirelessly as pit ponies in England and northern Europe. In the nineteenth century, many were imported to the United States to work in the Appalachian coal mines. These small but tough little horses were stabled underground. They worked long hours hauling coal, many never seeing the light of day. Only after they retired were they put to pasture in the green fields under an open sky. This practice lasted until the 1950s, when machines replaced horses. The defining characteristic of the American Miniature is its size. It must be shorter than thirty-four inches (86 cm) at the withers. American Miniatures today are used as show horses, pets, and therapy animals. Their small size fascinates and thrills all who see them.

Tiny jumpers. Show jumping has recently become a popular activity for American Miniatures. However, instead of riding the horse, the handler runs alongside of them! The fences are between one and two feet (30 and 60 cm) high, and the handler is not allowed to jump them.

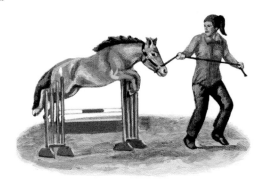

Clydesdale

The Clydesdale was developed in Scotland in the early 1700s. It comes from the Clyde Valley and was bred from local horses and imported Brabants from Belgium. The Clydesdale is a draft breed that was significantly influenced by the growth of the coal industry in Scotland. There was a need for a fast, strong draft horse that could haul coal where railroads couldn't reach. The Clydesdale filled this role with its long legs and naturally fast, high-stepping mobility. Its hard, flat, dinner-plate-sized hooves made it perfect for pulling heavy loads of coal quickly over great distances. The Clydesdale soon replaced the Shire in Scotland as the favored draft horse. In fact, it is such a popular heavy horse that it has been exported all over the globe. In Canada and the United States, the Clydesdale helped settle the West. And it is referred to as "the breed that built Australia," being the only draft horse used there until the twentieth century. Clydesdales are typically brown or bay, with long white feathering on their lower legs. *Cow hocks*, the turning in of the joints of the back of the leg (corresponding to the human ankle joints), are common in this breed.

American ambassadors. The most famous team of horses in North America is the Anheuser-Busch Clydesdales. These horses first appeared pulling the brewery's wagons in 1933, in celebration of the repeal of *Prohibition* (a law that forbade the manufacture, transportation, and sale of alcoholic beverages). The six-horse-hitch was able to pull one ton (0.9 metric ton) at a speed of five miles (8 km) per hour.

45

Connemara

The Connemara Pony is named after the district of the same name in western Ireland. It is a mixture of native Irish ponies and imported breeds – such as the Asian horses that arrived with Celtic tribes 2500 years ago and the Spanish and Barb horses brought by wealthy merchants in the sixteenth century. Life was difficult for the poor farmers of the rocky, mountainous coastland of the Connemara area. Most families had one mare, which pulled plow and cart and carried baskets called *creels*. These creels could hold heavy loads of rocks to clear land for farming, seaweed to fertilize the barren fields, and turf cut from bogs to be burned for heat and cooking. The horse also carted family members to church on Sundays. The Connemara's legs are short but strong and sturdy, helping it maneuver through muddy roads and sandy beaches. Its dense, waterproof coat helps it withstand storms that blow in from the Atlantic, sometimes for weeks on end. It has great stamina and survives on the tough grasses of its homeland. Possibly from centuries of scaling the craggy cliffs, the breed is known for its extraordinary jumping ability. Today, the Connemara is mostly used for riding and competitive jumping.

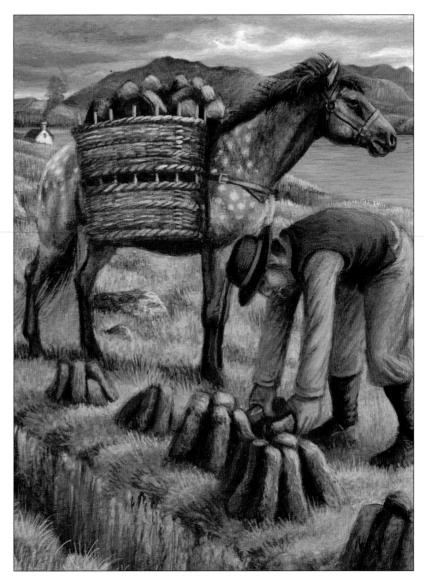

Cannon Ball! The most famous Connemara was a gray stallion named Cannon Ball. This farm horse regularly trotted home from market while his owner slept on the floor of the attached cart. Cannon Ball was also a local hero, winning the Farmer's Race at Oughterard sixteen years in a row, living up to his speedy name.

Brabant

Most large draft horses are descendants of the medieval Great Horse that carried armored knights into battle. The Brabant (pronounced breh-BONT), or Belgian Heavy Draft, is no exception. Belgium is a good place for raising horses. Its fertile soil and plentiful rain provide an ideal environment for abundant pasture, hay, and grain to grow, enabling farmers to raise these big, heavy horses. Brabants have short legs; thick, compact necks and bodies; and huge, muscular shoulders and quarters. These features gave them the power to pull plows through Belgium's heavy clay soils. Belgian farmers also used the Brabant for hauling bulky carts and wagons on the farm. In the sixteenth century, when most of Europe was breeding their draft horses to create smaller cavalry horses, Belgian farmers resisted. Instead, they kept the indispensable Brabant pure, and — when other countries returned to the need for massive draft horses — exported the Brabant for use as foundation stock. The Brabant breed is not only the heaviest draft horse, but it is also the most docile. Its personality is calm and willing, which makes it a well-behaved worker. It has a smaller, more refined head than most heavy breeds, and it is usually red or chestnut-colored, with some feathering on its lower legs.

Green horse? Many present-day farmers and loggers are returning to old-time methods, using horses because they are more ecofriendly than machinery. Horses don't pollute the air like tractors, and the manure makes instant fertilizer. They are also quieter and don't require gas or diesel fuel — horses run on hay!

Canadian Horse

French settlers arrived in Canada in the early seventeenth century. In 1665, King Louis XIV began sending shipments of horses from France to the settlers in order to establish a breeding program. These horses were leased to the colonists in exchange for money or foals. After three years, the leased horses became the property of the farmer. The Canadian Horse played a vital role in the colonists' lives, clearing land and farming it, carrying children to school, pulling crop cutters and carriages, and providing entertainment through racing. Even though they worked so hard, these horses lived in difficult conditions. They labored long hours, and their owners made no special effort to feed or shelter them through the brutal winters. The French practice was to *dock*, or cut, the horses' tails. This ensured that their tails would not get caught in farm equipment, but it left the horses with no way to protect themselves from the mosquitoes and flies that plagued them in the summers. As the horses survived and reproduced, offspring became smaller and tougher, earning them the nickname "The Little Iron Horse." The Canadian Horse was named the National Horse of Canada in 2002, in recognition of the contribution the breed made to the development of its country.

Making the cut. Cutting is a popular sport in Canada. A cutting competition is similar to the work that farmers do on ranches, when individual cows must be *cut*, or separated, from the herd. In the arena, the rider does not touch the reins, letting the horse work instinctively to control the cow. A Canadian Cutting Horse may be any breed, but it must have balance, agility, and cow sense.

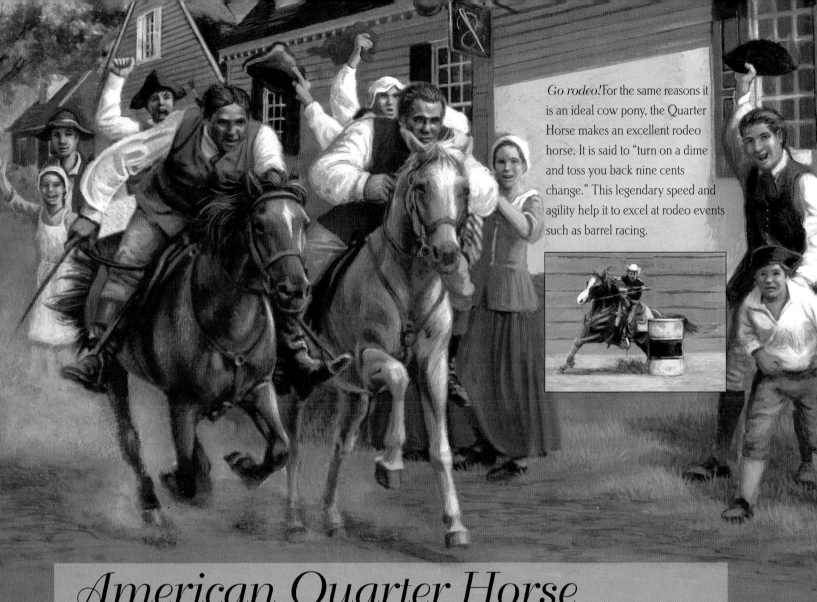

Go rodeo! For the same reasons it is an ideal cow pony, the Quarter Horse makes an excellent rodeo horse. It is said to "turn on a dime and toss you back nine cents change." This legendary speed and agility help it to excel at rodeo events such as barrel racing.

American Quarter Horse

The horses of the original English settlers of America mixed with Spanish horses purchased from Native Americans to produce the Quarter Horse. The American colonists used these horses for all types of work, such as hauling lumber to the mill, pulling plows, and drawing carriages to church. These early colonists were also fans of horse racing. They raced their horses wherever they could, be it across open field or down a town street. Quarter Horses are named for their ability to race the quarter-mile (0.4 km) stretch, since they can go very fast over this short distance, bolting from a standing start. When the Thoroughbred was introduced to the United States in the 1800s, long-distance racing became the sport of choice. By this time, though, the Quarter Horse had become popular as a cow pony with the pioneers of the West. The breed's explosive speed, agility, and cow sense made it ideal for working large herds of cattle on the open range. The Quarter Horse's power comes from its muscular hindquarters. It is a compact horse with a short head and small muzzle. The Quarter Horse has the most extensive breed registry in the world today, with over three million registered animals. Most are found in the cattle-rich countries of Australia, Canada, and the United States.

Bashkir

The Bashkir is an ancient breed from the Bashkiria area on the southern slopes of the Ural Mountains in southern Russia. The nomadic Bashkiria peoples use their horses for many purposes, such as transportation and draft work. The horses are also a source of food, providing meat and milk. The Bashkir's milk has a higher fat content than other breeds. This helps the foals to develop an extra insulating layer of fat, a characteristic feature of this breed, enabling it to cope with living in one of the coldest regions of the world. Bashkirs also have stocky builds, short legs, and large heads with small nostrils (for conserving body heat). Their most distinguishing trait is their long, thick winter coat, which is sometimes curly. The Bashkiria peoples weave blankets and clothing from the horses' luxurious manes, tails, and coats. This breed is incredibly hardy, living outside year-round, even in subzero temperatures. These horses can even find food under three feet (0.9 m) of snow, by digging with their hooves. The Bashkir has great endurance and can pull troikas for long distances in deep snow.

Mare's milk. A Bashkir mare produces as many as 550 gallons (2082 L) of milk in a season (April through August)! The Bashkiria peoples use the milk to make dairy products such as cheese and a fermented drink called *koumiss*, which is a staple of the local diet and has been used as a medicine in greater Russia to treat various ailments.

Bashkiria Ural Mountains RUSSIA

Camargue

In the south of France is a marshy area of the Rhone river delta called the Camargue (pronounced CA-margh). The Camargue Horse has lived here since prehistoric times. This "Horse of the Sea" often stands or runs, knee-deep in saltwater, in the flooded delta. It is a very hardy horse that eats tough grasses and reeds and drinks *brackish* water (a mixture of saltwater and freshwater). The summers in this area are hot, humid, and full of biting insects. The winters are very cold, with fast winds whipping across the open marsh. French *gardians*, or cowboys, ride the Camargues to herd the equally tough black Camargue cattle. Camargue Horses are born brown or black. As they mature, their hair turns white, though their skin remains dark. These small, compact horses have heavy heads with short necks and stocky legs. Their hooves rarely need to be shod. Today, Camargue Horses mainly reside in the Camargue Regional Park. They are often used as trail horses for tourists through the area.

Name brand horse.
The Camargue Horses roam through the marshes of the nature reserve in semi-wild herds called *manades*. To keep track of the horses, gardians brand them on their left hindquarters according to the year they were born.

Equine Entertainment

When was the first time two men argued over whose horse was the fastest? The answer has been lost in time, but surely it happened soon after they began riding horses, making racing the earliest type of equine entertainment. These contests have come in many forms – from short- to long-distance, from fixed tracks to cross-country, and from horses racing solo to teams driving wagons. Chariot races were as popular in the arenas of ancient Greece and Rome as modern-day *sulky* races are on the tracks of Russia and the United States (a sulky is a light, two-wheeled carriage ridden by one person and pulled by one horse).

When working horses weren't laboring on the battlefield, farm field, or city street, they were putting their skills to the test for the entertainment of people. Of the dozens of equestrian sports, most are derived from the practical tasks that horses performed for their masters. Hunting on horseback (a necessity of survival before it became a sport) evolved into sport jumping and cross-country racing; pulling farm equipment became the sport of weight pulling; and the work of ranch hands developed into rodeos.

THE THOROUGHBRED, A RACING BREED.

THE AZTECA, DEMONSTRATES CATTLE HORSE SKILLS FOR SPORT.

52

THE LIPIZZAN, A DRESSAGE BREED.

THE FALABELLA, BRED TO BE A PET.

It takes intense training and cooperation for any horse-and-human team to excel. But in no sport is that relationship more important than in *dressage*. Evolving from cavalry training, dressage developed in the riding schools of Europe during the Renaissance, where riders control their horses with barely perceptible signals and exhibit the skills of their steeds in a graceful and stylish fashion. Dressage horses need to be calm, flexible, and strong. Dressage is often compared to dance. It is seen not only in competitions, but also in bullfighting arenas and at circuses.

Some horses are bred for their personalities or for physical appearances rather than for their functional or competitive skills. The upper class, who could afford to keep horses as pets, developed miniature horses to serve as curiosities and companions. Today, miniatures are not only novelties, they are also bred for recreational purposes such as the show ring and as children's mounts. Even some medium-sized horses are bred for their personalities or coat types rather than for their working skills.

Thoroughbred

The Thoroughbred is the fastest distance-running horse in the world. It was developed in England in the seventeenth and eighteenth centuries for the sport of kings. All Thoroughbreds can be traced back to three Arabian *sires* (male parents) imported from the Middle East: Darley, Godolphin, and Byerly. These three stallions were bred with native sprinting mares. After much selective breeding, a horse of superior speed, power, and endurance was produced. The Thoroughbred's physical features reflect these three functions. The horse's legs are lengthy and strong, the deep chest holds large lungs and heart, and the head is straight and lean with big, flaring nostrils for greater airflow. For balance, the Thoroughbred's muscular, streamlined body and neck are long. Its skin is fine and "dry," like its desert ancestors, for quick cooling. For over three hundred years, only the fastest horses have been bred. Because they were created strictly for racing, without consideration for their personalities, Thoroughbreds are known to be high-strung and unstable, needing skilled handlers and riders. Developed to mature early, some horses race at just two years of age.

A racing heart! Secretariat was one of the fastest racehorses in history. In the 1973 Belmont Stakes in New York, he finished an astounding thirty-one lengths (about 250 ft, or 75 m) in front of his closest competitor, setting a world record that still stands today. Secretariat's giant heart — weighing almost twenty-two pounds (10 kg), or thirteen pounds (5.9 kg) heavier than the average Thoroughbred — gave him the stamina he needed to win.

Standardbred

The Standardbred is a breed developed to race in harness at a trot, rather than under saddle at a gallop. American colonists developed this breed in the eighteenth century using Morgans, Thoroughbreds, and Canadian and American trotters and pacers. Trotting and pacing are fast yet smooth gaits. The trot is a *diagonal gait*, in which the legs move in diagonal pairs. The pace is a *lateral gait*, in which the legs on the same side move together. In 1879, the name "Standardbred" was given to the breed, due to the fact that registered horses had to be able to trot a mile (1.6 km) within the "standard" time of two minutes and thirty seconds. Today, it is quite common for the Standardbred, the fastest horse in harness, to trot or pace that same distance in under two minutes. The Standardbred resembles the Thoroughbred, but it has shorter legs and a sturdier build. A notable feature of this breed is that the *croup* (highpoint of the hindquarters) is an inch or two (2.5 or 5 cm) higher than the withers. This, combined with the powerful quarters, gives the horse added thrust. Harness racing requires that the animal's legs, joints, and hooves are soundly constructed and that it is able to run perfectly straight.

Hobble horse. In harness racing, a horse breaking from its trot or pace into a gallop must move to the outside of the track and resume its gait, almost always resulting in a loss. To prevent this from happening, pacers are fixed with a *hobble*, a harness connecting the front leg above the knee to the hock of the rear leg.

Swiss Warmblood

As early as 964 AD, an order of Benedictine monks at the Monastery of Einsiedeln in Switzerland bred native horses for use as practical farm horses. Switzerland is a mountainous country, so the breed, named Einsiedler, was adapted to rugged terrain and cold winters. This made it a good mount and pack animal for the Swiss Army. (Even in the present day, the Swiss Army uses the Einsiedler for its mounted cavalry troops and as animal transport units.) In the 1960s, the Einsiedler was crossbred with many other breeds and reinvented as an all-purpose sporting horse, named the Swiss Warmblood. It is now bred at the Swiss Federal Stud at Avenches. Selection for breeding of the Swiss Warmblood is very strict. Stallions must pass performance tests at ages three-and-a-half and five to be allowed to breed, and mares are tested at age three. These tests include dressage, jumping, cross-country riding, and *driving* (pulling a cart or carriage). The tall, elegant Swiss Warmblood makes an excellent sports competitor. It is well proportioned and athletic, and it comes in all colors.

Too hot to handle! Hotblood is a name given to desert-type horses that are suited to hot climates and have fiery temperaments. *Cold-blood* refers to heavy draft breeds of northern Europe, with bodies suited to cold climates and having cool temperaments. A *warmblood* is a cross between the two.

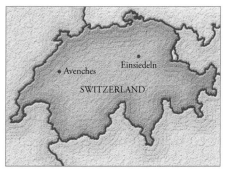

57

Azteca

Mexico has a long tradition of cattle ranching, which was brought over by the Spanish in the sixteenth century. After the Mexican Revolution in 1910, the *charros*, or Mexican cowboys, began holding *charreadas* to preserve and promote their traditions. The charreada is the original rodeo, in which charros show off the skills they use in their jobs by competing in events such as calf roping, bronco riding, and horsemanship. Mexicans take considerable pride in the charreada, wearing traditional costumes and celebrating their cultural heritage. In the 1970s, a group of Mexican organizations set out to create a breed of horse for the charreada that would represent Mexico and resemble the Spanish conquistadores' horses. They created the Azteca in 1972 by crossing Andalusians for their elegant look, Quarter Horses for their speed and strength, and hardy Criollos for their historical importance as the mount of Mexican revolutionaries. The Azteca is the perfect charro horse: flashy and stylish, and quick enough to keep ahead of cattle. It is also the proper height for its rider to take down a bull by the tail, and its strength, balance, and agility enable the rider to rope and hold wild mares. The Azteca was the first breed to be created in Mexico and is now the country's national horse.

Buckin' broncos! The term *bronco* originally referred to a wild or untrained horse that bucked its rider. The sport of bronco riding developed in charreadas and rodeos to demonstrate the cowboy's job of taming these horses. Today, horses are bred specifically for their bucking ability and for competition in these events.

Lusitano

The Lusitano (pronounced LUH-see-tan-oh), from Portugal, is very similar to the Spanish Andalusian, and both were once known as Iberian horses. When not being ridden as steeds in battle, Iberian horses were used for mounted bullfights and dressage. In the 1600s, the Spanish stopped fighting bulls from horseback and began to breed their horses for traits that made them good riding horses. The Portuguese, however, continued the practice of mounted bullfights and kept breeding their horses for traditional traits. The agility and courage that made the Iberian horse a skilled warrior also helped it to succeed in the bullring. In between charges of the bull, the horse often calmly completes dressage moves. In 1966, a distinction was finally officially recognized between the Andalusian and Lusitano breeds. In its homeland today, breeding of the Lusitano is still mainly influenced by its job as a bullfighter. As any Lusitano owner will tell you, a horse that willingly fights a bull and doesn't run away makes a loyal, brave mount.

Backstabbers! In Portuguese-style bullfighting, the first stage is fought by a *cavaleiro*, or horseman. The cavaleiro's job is to stab the bull's back with three or four *bandarilhas*, or small javelins. In the second stage, eight men charge and subdue the bull. Unlike Spanish bullfighting, the bull is not killed in the Portuguese bullring.

Lipizzan

Leaping Lipizzans! The three primary leaps performed by Lipizzans are the *levade*, in which the horse sits back on deeply bent hind legs, rearing up with forelegs tucked underneath; the *courbette*, in which the horse, starting from levade, springs forward on its hind legs with the front legs still lifted; and the *capriole*, in which the horse leaps high into the air from levade, with all legs off of the ground.

The Spanish Riding School in Vienna was founded in 1572 and is the oldest riding academy in the world. The Austro-Hungarian Empire established the academy to train nobility in the art of riding. Although the school is in Vienna, it was named "Spanish" after the original horses ridden there. The Spanish Riding School now exclusively uses Lipizzans (pronounced Lip-it-SANS), named for the stud at Lipizza, now part of Slovenia. The stud was founded in 1580 by Austrian Archduke Charles II in order to breed riding and light-carriage horses. Lipizzans lived on a rocky limestone plateau, which, through natural selection, created a breed with hard hooves and strong bones. These features were necessary for the movements of *Haute École*, or "High School," of dressage, meaning the highest level of training. It takes seven years to fully train a Lipizzan to perform the ballet-like movements of Haute École. Other features of this compact horse include very powerful limbs, haunches, and hindquarters; a short neck; and a lofty, rhythmic action in their legs. Lipizzans are slow to mature, but they are long-lived, often performing into their twenties and living into their thirties. The breed is famous for its white coat, although other colors sometimes appear. At birth, Lipizzans are brown or black, turning white as they mature.

61

Knabstrupper

In 1808, a Danish judge purchased a spotted mare of Spanish ancestry that had been brought to Denmark by Spanish cavalry during the Napoleonic Wars. The judge bred this mare with a Frederiksborg stallion (another Danish breed of Spanish descent) at his estate at Knabstrupgaard. The spotting gene is dominant, so it was possible for this one mare to pass on the gene to an entire breed of colorful horses, which are usually white with brown or black spots. The Knabstrupper (pronounced cugh-NOB-strewp-er) evolved into a carriage horse of great speed and stamina. Because of its spotted coat and ability to learn quickly, it also became a popular circus entertainer; its broad back gave acrobats a wide base on which to perform. Since it was bred only for its coat color, the quality of the breed started to deteriorate in the nineteenth century. (Breeding only for color doesn't take into consideration other features, such as the animal's health or temperament, which can lead to poor physical condition or disposition in offspring.) Also, the Knabstrupper numbers were few, which led to problems of inbreeding. In 1971, a Danish Knabstrupper association imported three Appaloosa stallions to Denmark to introduce new blood to the breed. This was a good mix because both the Knabstrupper and the Appaloosa are of Spanish descent and carry the spotted gene. Today, the Knabstrupper is still used as a riding and circus horse.

Trick riding. The modern-day equestrian sport *vaulting* evolved from circus trick riding. A rider, or a team of riders, performs acrobatic moves on the back of a horse as it canters in a circle. The horse, usually a heavy draft, must be calm with a wide, flat back.

Nature or nurture? Most miniature horses are scaled down in size by selective breeding. However, the Guoxia's small dimensions seem to have evolved from natural selection, adapting to its harsh environment as most ponies do. The Guoxia is one of only two naturally developing miniature horse breeds (the other is the Caspian).

RUSSIA

MONGOLIA

CHINA

INDIA

Guoxia

The Guoxia (pronounced GOO-shee-ah) is an ancient breed found in southwest China. It lives in a mountainous area with a cold, rainy climate. This very hardy miniature horse has a thick mane, tail, and coat for warmth. The name "Guoxia" translates from Chinese to "under fruit tree horse," which hints to one of its original uses. The horse stood in orchards under the fruit trees so that harvesters could drop the picked fruit into the baskets that it carried on its back. In the Han dynasty, these horses were playthings of the wives and concubines of nobility. They served as pets for the amusement of later emperors and their courts as well. The Guoxia is only ten hands high, or forty inches (102 cm) at the withers. Though it is small enough to be classified as a pony, it has horse proportions and characteristics. For years, the Guoxia was thought to have become extinct. The only proof that it once existed was its image in sculptures and carvings. Then, in 1981, Chinese officials discovered a herd of about one thousand Guoxias in the mountains, and a breed association was immediately formed to protect them. Today, the Guoxia is used for pulling carts and for entertainment at children's parks.

Falabella

In nineteenth-century Argentina, an Irish rancher named Patrick Newell bought several of the smallest horses from a Criollo herd owned by the indigenous Mapuches. Criollos were the descendants of Andalusians brought to South America by the Spaniards. These *feral* horses (domestic animals that live in the wild) grazed the grasslands of the Pampas, enduring strong sun, sudden storms, limited water, and hungry pumas. This environment forced them to adapt, and through natural selection they evolved into a hardy horse. Mr. Newell and his son-in-law, Juan Falabella, selectively bred these small Criollos over several generations, producing miniature offspring. Some little European horses were introduced into the line, including Shetland ponies, and Patrick and Juan ended up with a herd of horses averaging thirty inches (76 cm) tall. The Falabella is bred to be a miniature horse and not a pony. Because they were created as pets, they have gentle and friendly personalities. Falabellas are not meant to be ridden, but some can pull light vehicles. These horses are very long-lived, often surviving to age forty or forty-five. The Falabella is the world's smallest breed of horse. At birth, the foals measure about twelve inches (31 cm) in height. They reach their full size by age three.

Which is bigger: a dog or a horse? "Horse" might seem the obvious answer, but not necessarily when compared to the Falabella. This miniature breed measures around thirty inches tall (76 cm) and weighs up to one hundred pounds (45 kg), while a large dog such as the Irish Wolfhound is at least thirty-two inches (81 cm) tall and over 120 pounds (54 kg).

North American Curly Horse

Curly-coated horses have been documented all over the world and throughout history. Entire breeds of curly-haired horses had never been encountered, but occasionally a curly-haired horse appeared. From the 1800s in North America, the Sioux tribe prized curly horses as sacred mounts for their chief and medicine men. In the early 1900s, a rancher in Nevada noticed a few curly-coated horses among a wild Mustang herd on his land. After a very hard winter, the rancher saw that the "Curlies" (as they came to be known) were the only survivors. He caught and introduced several of them into his own herd. When he bred them with other breeds, he found that the curly-hair trait had transferred to the offspring. This unique coat type is still being studied today and has been found to appear on a dominant and a *recessive* gene (a gene that doesn't present unless inherited from both parents); the curly coats that appear occasionally in other populations are due to the recessive gene. This coat can also come in different varieties. Some horses have only a wavy mane and tail, and curly hair on the lower legs and inner ears, while others have tight curls all over, which sometimes shed completely out in the summer, leaving the horses bald! Curlies, being of Mustang stock, are very tough and intelligent. Though they are bred strictly for their curly coats, they are able competitors in a variety of sports.

Achoo! The North American Curly Horse is claimed to be the only hypoallergenic breed of horse. People who are usually allergic to horses can often handle and ride Curlies without a serious allergic reaction. This may be due to the lack of a sneeze-inducing protein in the Curly's coat.

Feral Horses

All over the world, there are populations of horses that live in the wild. These horses are called feral. Though they live like wild horses, they are actually descended from domestic horses that escaped or were turned loose, survived, and learned to live on their own.

Feral horse populations are often controversial because they can have a negative effect on the environment, for example by trampling vegetation and compacting soil. Also, since there aren't usually any natural predators to these herds, their numbers can get out of control. If there isn't enough food for all of the horses, some may die of starvation. To deal with this, governments often get involved in caring for the horses or in managing their populations.

THE BRUMBY, A FERAL BREED.

66

Chincoteague

Chincoteague (pronounced SHING-keh-teeg) and Assateague islands are sandy, marshy islands that lie off the coast of Virginia. The Chincoteague Pony most likely originated from horses that were let loose here by American colonists in the seventeenth century. These hardy ponies have survived for centuries out in the open, withstanding fierce Atlantic storms, hot summers, poor grazing conditions, and little fresh water. By the early 1900s, this pony group started to deteriorate, with foals born stunted and distorted. In the 1920s, the Chincoteague Volunteer Fire Department started managing the herd. They introduced Welsh and Shetland ponies, along with *pinto* (white with colored patches) Mustangs, to upgrade the Chincoteague herd. Every year on the last Wednesday and Thursday of July, the fire department holds Pony Penning Days. Local ranchers, known as "saltwater cowboys," round up the horses on Assateague Island and guide them across a shallow channel of water to Chincoteague Island. Some of the foals are auctioned off to keep the herd size manageable and to raise funds for the care of the ponies. This has become a popular tourist attraction and is accompanied by a carnival and weeklong festivities.

Famous foal. After attending Pony Penning Day in 1946 and buying one of the foals, Marguerite Henry wrote a children's book about her foal, which she had named Misty. *Misty of Chincoteague* was published in 1947 and, along with its movie adaptation, made Chincoteague Ponies famous. The real-life Misty later toured the world, meeting children.

Mustang

Mustangs are feral horses that developed from stock brought to North America by the Spanish in the 1500s. As the West was settled, different horses from various breeds escaped from, or were turned out by, the pioneers, and these horses joined and mated with some of the Mustang herds. By 1900, there was an estimated two million feral Mustangs in the United States. With such large numbers, they competed with cattle for grazing on public lands, so ranchers took action. Mustangs were slaughtered and sold to the meat industry until there were only approximately seventeen thousand and three hundred remaining in the mid-twentieth century. In 1959, the United States Congress passed a law protecting Mustangs, and, in 1971, the horses were declared an endangered species. It is now illegal to capture or harm Mustangs, which Congress referred to as "living symbols of the historic and pioneer spirit of the West." The United States Bureau of Land Management regularly captures some Mustangs, often using helicopters, and offers them for adoption – to keep the populations at a manageable size. Mustangs are a very hardy, intelligent breed, a result of adaptation to living in the wild for centuries.

The real deal. Throughout western Canada and the United States, there are isolated herds of Mustangs that are direct descendents of those first Spanish horses, horses that have never intermingled with other breeds. Associations have been formed to ensure the purity of these herds, such as the Suffield Mustangs of Alberta and the Spanish Mustangs of Wyoming.

Brumby

Feral foe. With over three hundred thousand Brumbies, Australia has the largest feral horse population of any country. In addition to feral horses, there are also feral pigs, cattle, water buffaloes, camels, and donkeys roaming the outback. These animals all compete for resources with native animals, such as kangaroos and wallabies.

The first horses arrived in Australia with European settlers in 1788. These horses were imported to do an array of jobs, from herding on the immense cattle ranches and sheep stations to doing draft work on farms and in cities. Some of these horses escaped or were set free in the vast Australian outback. The outback, covering 70 percent of the continent, is extremely hot and arid. The horses adapted to these difficult conditions, becoming tough and rugged. The feral Brumbies, likely named after an Australian soldier, multiplied into the thousands. This became a problem because the horses competed with Australia's natural wildlife for limited food and water. The Australian government started a program in the 1960s of *culling*, or killing, Brumbies to control their population. The feral horses were shot from helicopters and jeeps. This was very controversial and the culling of the herds is still hotly debated today. Brumbies are sometimes captured for work or the meat industry, but they are seldom used for riding because they are hard to tame and not the most attractive of horses. The Brumby has a heavy head, upright shoulders, and cow hocks.

Sable Island Pony

Sable Island is a twenty-mile (32-km) long, crescent-shaped sandbank located one hundred miles (161 km) east of Nova Scotia, Canada, in the Atlantic Ocean. It is home to seals, seabirds, and the Sable Island Pony. Sable Island is surrounded by constantly shifting sand shoals, the cause of many shipwrecks. The ponies could possibly have been shipwreck survivors, but it is more likely that they were left on the island by eighteenth-century settlers, who occupied a base there for assisting stranded sailors. The horses are probably of French or Spanish origin. The island has no trees and is covered mainly by grasses and shrubs. The Sable Island Ponies eat this plant life and get water from freshwater ponds or by digging their own water holes in the sand. They find shelter from Atlantic storms and bitter winds by positioning themselves between the high sand dunes and hills, especially in winter when the polar ice surrounds the island. These tough ponies are stocky, with short, strong legs for moving through sand. In the past, ponies were captured and taken by boat to the mainland for auction, but since 1961, the horses have been protected by law and now experience no human interference whatsoever.

Feral families. The Sable Island Pony herd ranges from two to three hundred animals. They roam the island in family groups of four to eight individuals. A dominant stallion, followed by one or more mares and their offspring, usually leads a unit. Bachelor males sometimes form their own groups.

Conclusion

There are over fifty-eight million horses in the world today. They show great variety in shape, color, size, and specialized features. From tiny miniature horses to massive draft breeds, humans have shaped the way horses look, act, and live. But these magnificent creatures have also changed our lives in drastic ways. Because of horses, we live, travel, fight, work, and play differently than we did before they entered our lives. Machines have taken over many of the roles that horses once filled, and today's horses are mainly used for ceremonial, competitive, or recreational purposes. But whether you own a horse, compete in equestrian sports, ride trails on horseback, or just like reading about our equine friends, you can see how special the relationship is between human and horse.

Bibliography

BOOKS

Arthus-Bertrand, Yann. *Horses.* New York: Artisan, 2008.

Baquedano, Elizabeth. *Eyewitness Books: Aztec, Inca & Maya.* New York: Dorling Kindersley, 1993.

Clutton-Brock, Juliet. *Eyewitness Books: Horse.* New York: Alfred A. Knopf, 1992.

Costantino, Maria. *The Handbook of Horse Breeds.* England: Silverdale Books, 2003.

Edwards, Elwyn Hartley. *The Encyclopedia of the Horse.* New York: Dorling Kindersley, 2008.

Gravett, Christopher. *Eyewitness Books: Knight.* New York: Alfred A. Knopf, 1993.

Hendricks, Bonnie. *International Encyclopedia of Horse Breeds.* Norman: University of Oklahoma Press, 2007.

McBane, Susan. *The Illustrated Encyclopedia of Horse Breeds.* New Jersey: Wellfleet Press, 1997.

Murdoch, David. *Eyewitness Books: North American Indian.* New York: Dorling Kindersley, 1995.

Tucker, Louise. *The Visual Dictionary of the Horse.* New York: Dorling Kindersley, 1994.

ARTICLES

Bahls, Jane Easter. "Horsepower Logging." *American Forests,* January/February 1991, 49-50.

Chapin, Pam. "Animals Are Eco-friendly." *Countryside & Small Stock Journal,* May/June 2004, 101-102.

Goodman, Patricia L. "The Terrific Trakehner." *Horse Illustrated,* October 1983.

Grutz, Jane Waldron. "The Barb." *Saudi Aramco World,* January/February 2007, 8-17.

Hynes, Patricia. "Mongolian Trotting – Personal Narrative." *Contemporary Review,* July 1993, 39-40.

Martin, John D. "Sports and Games in Icelandic Saga Literature." *Scandinavian Studies* 75 (2003): 27-32.

McCarthy, Brenda, editor. "Gentle Giants: The Clydesdales." *Blaze Magazine* 22 (2008): 14-15.

———. "Unsung Heroes: The Canadian Horse." *Blaze Magazine* 23 (2009): 12-13.

Peck, Robert McCracken. "Home Again! – Mongolian Horse Population." *International Wildlife,* September/October 1999, 35-41.

Trut, Lyudmila N. "Early Canid Domestication: The Farm-Fox Experiment." *American Scientist,* March/April 1999, 160-69.

WEB SITES

• American Drum Horse Association, "Drum Horse History," www.drumhorseassociation.com/drumhorsehistory.htm

• American Knabstrupper Association, "About the Knabstrupper," http://www.knabstruppers.com

• American Museum of Natural History, "The Horse," http://www.amnh.org/exhibitions/horse

• Autry National Center, "Art of the Charrería: A Mexican Tradition," http://www.autrynationalcenter.org/explore/exhibits/charreria.html

• Budweiser, "The Great American Tradition," http://www.budweiser.com/en/world-of-budweiser/clydesdales/default.aspx#/en/world-of-budweiser/clydesdales/american-icons.aspx

• Caspian Horse Society of the Americas, "Caspian History," http://www.caspian.org/about-caspians/caspian-history.asp

• *Equine Journal,* "Back to the Future: Baroque Breeds in Modern Times," http://www.equinejournal.com/articles/back-to-the-future-baroque-breeds-in-modern-times

• Equiworld, "Azteca: El Caballo Supremo," http://www.equiworld.net/horses/horsecare/Breeds/azteca/index.htm

• Equiworld, "The Bashkir," http://www.equiworld.com/ssa/bashkir/index.htm

• Equiworld, "The Fjord Horse," http://www.equiworld.com/ssa/fjord/index.htm

• ESPN, "Secretariat remains No. 1 name in racing," http://espn.go.com/sportscentury/features/00016464.html

• Falabella Miniature Horse Association, "FMHA'S Official Web Site," http://www.falabellafmha.com

• Food and Agriculture Organization of the United Nations, "The State of the Basotho Pony in Lesotho," http://www.fao.org/docrep/006/Y3970E/y3970e08.htm

• Horse Show Central, "Brabant – Horse Breeds & Info," http://www.horseshowcentral.com/draught_horse/brabant/364/1

• International Curly Horse Organization, "Discussion of the Inheritance of Curly Hair in Horses," www.curlyhorses.org/index.php?page=68

• International Curly Horse Organization, "Frequently Asked Questions about the Curly Horse," http://www.curlyhorses.org/index.php?page=faqcurly

• International Museum of the Horse, "Horse Breeds of the World," http://www.imh.org/horse-breeds-of-the-world

• International Museum of the Horse, "Legacy of the Horse," http://www.imh.org/legacy-of-the-horse

• Iran Chamber Society, "History of Iran," http://www.iranchamber.com/history/achaemenids/arrian_battle_of_gaugamela.php

• Kladruber Breeding Farm Inc, "Breed and History," http://www.kladrubers.com/index.php?pages=hisofbr

• Kristull Ranch, "History: Royal Connection," http://www.caspianhorse.com/history_royal.htm

• Malealea Lodge and Pony Trek Centre, "Basotho Pony," http://www.malealea.com/basuto-pony.html

• Sable Island Green Horse Society, "Sable Island Horses," http://www.greenhorsesociety.com/Horses/Horses.htm